Published by Ladybird Books Ltd 2014
A Penguin Company
Penguin Books Ltd, 80 Strand, London, WC2R 0RL, UK
Penguin Books Australia Ltd, Camberwell, Victoria, Australia
Penguin Books (NZ), 67 Apollo Drive, Rosedale, Auckland 0632,
New Zealand(a division of Pearson New Zealand Ltd)

www.ladybird.com

ISBN: 978-0-72329-126-8
001 - 10 9 8 7 6 5 4 3 2 1
Printed in Poland

THE OFFICIAL ANNUAL 2015

CONTENTS

Odd Squad

It's a busy day at the LEGO® CITY police station with all of those crooks around! But some other odd things are going on too. Look closely at the picture and see if you can spot the five things that just don't fit in.

Drive Time

It's time for the big race! Can you help racing driver Jazz Peterson work out the best route round the track so that he can pick up all the trophies along the way? Colour in the car to make it ready for the race. Three . . . two . . . one . . . GO!

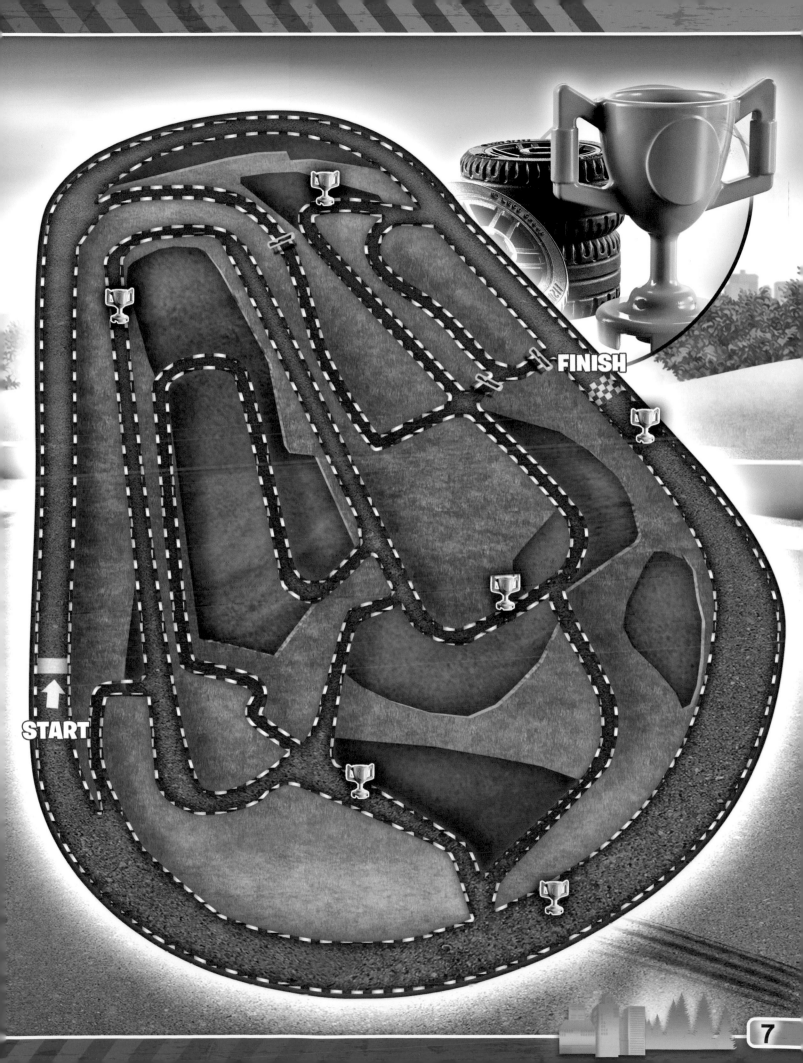

FINISH

START

On Guard!

No matter what the day throws at them, the LEGO CITY coast guard patrol are always ready! How much equipment do you think they need for the day ahead? Write how many there are of each item in the empty boxes.

COAST GUARD

Mechanic Panic

This mechanic thought that removing the monster truck's wheel would be a piece of cake – until it rolled off and landed beside a pile of spares! Follow the line to work out which wheel is his.

TURBO

LF60055

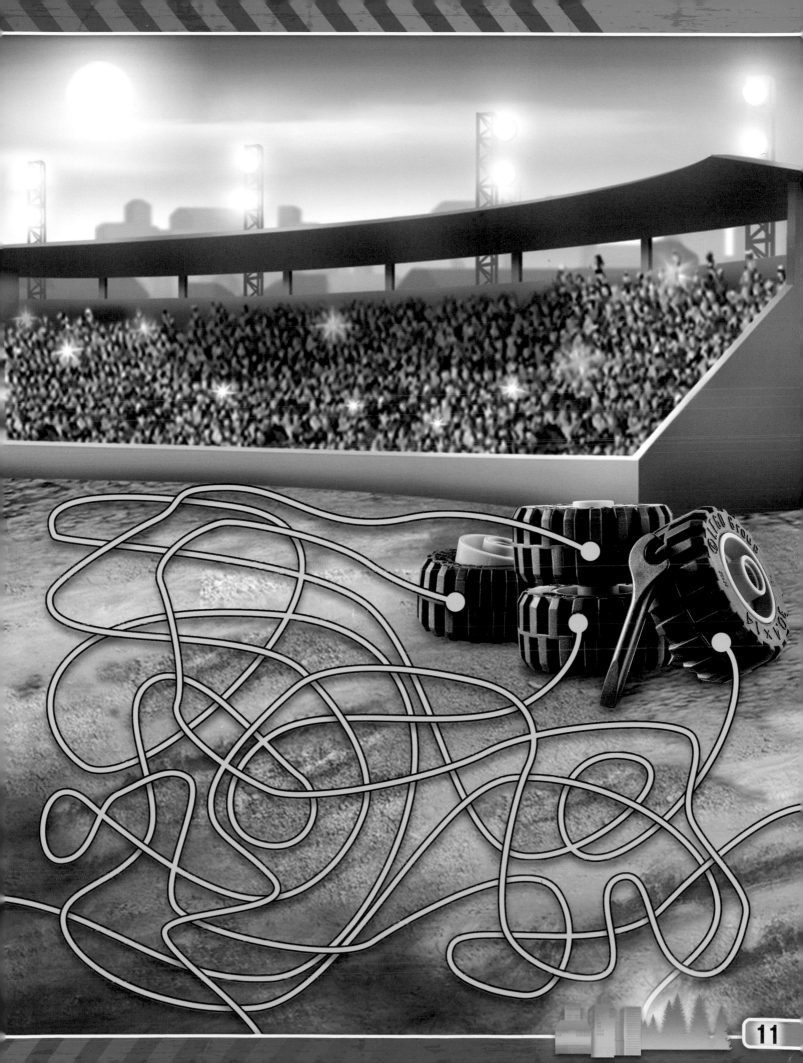

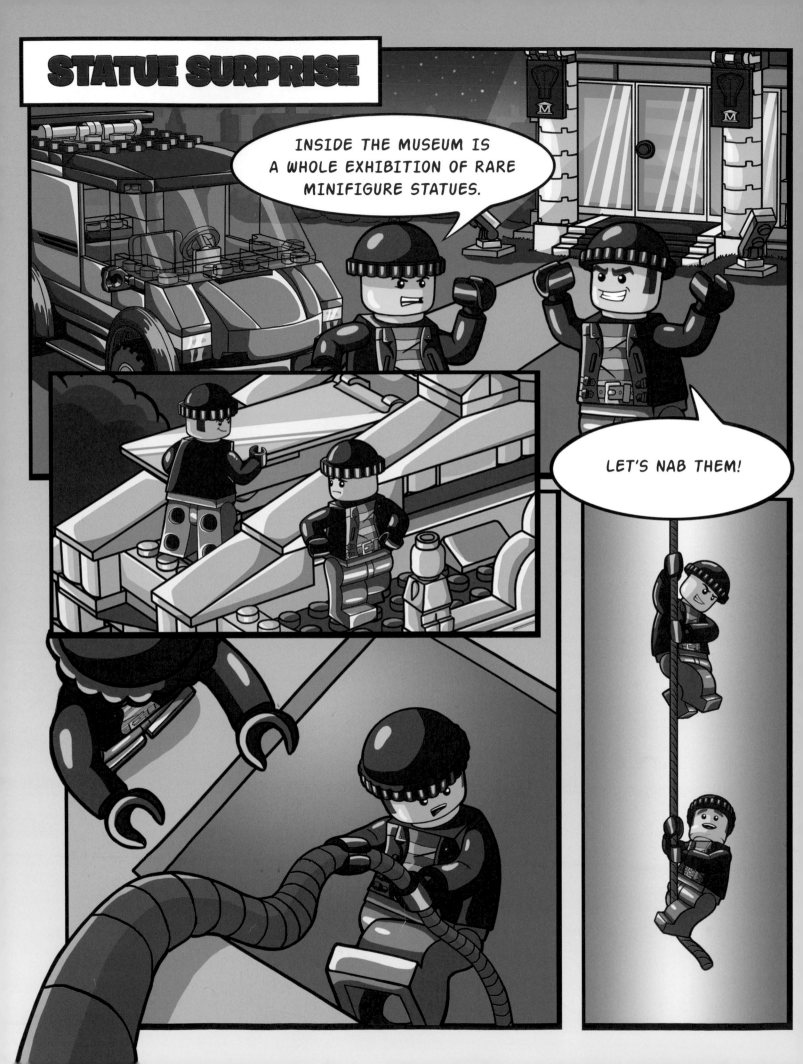

Flame Game

Here is the LEGO CITY fire brigade's report on a recent emergency at the airport. Can you tell which of the three photos matches what has been written in the report?

Fire Report

Fire! Fire! Two of our brave firefighters arrived quickly on the scene when a plane's engine caught fire. While one of them jumped out and grabbed the hose, the other climbed onto the roof to use the water cannon. Together, they both fired water at the burning engine and saved the day.

Photo no.

Arctic Drop-Off

It's getting foggy out there at base camp! This helicopter has arrived to drop off supplies, but the explorers can barely see it in the Arctic conditions. Can you see which silhouette is the correct one?

Icy Cargo

The Arctic explorers use dogs to help them carry their cargo (and themselves!) across the snow and ice. It takes one dog to carry each object. How many dogs are needed for each of the examples on the page opposite?

ARCTIC-1

Stolen Treasure

The King's Knights are trying to stop the Dragon Soldier from getting away with the stolen treasure! Match the numbers to the missing parts of the picture to complete the action scene.

Dragon's Gold

The King's Knights have launched a surprise attack on the evil Dragon Wizard, who has kidnapped their princess! While the Knights attempt to rescue her, see if you can count how many coins the dragon has spilled from its stolen treasure chest.

Ambush!

Back in the forest, a pair of the King's Knights are taking the treasure back to the King – but they have been ambushed by Dragon Soldiers!
One of the pictures on the page opposite is a mirror image of this scene.
Can you tell which one?

1

2

3

4

Under Siege

Dragon Soldiers have surrounded the King's castle!
The brave White Knight has charged out over the drawbridge to do battle.
Which of the five shadows matches him?

Gatehouse Raid

The King's gatehouse is also under attack! Soldiers from both sides have joined the battle, but one is missing. Can you work out which one it is?

Party Masks

Island Warrior is holding a massive party and has asked all of his guests to wear decorated masks, just like his. Help Barbarian and Tomahawk Warrior to decorate their masks so that they can arrive in style!

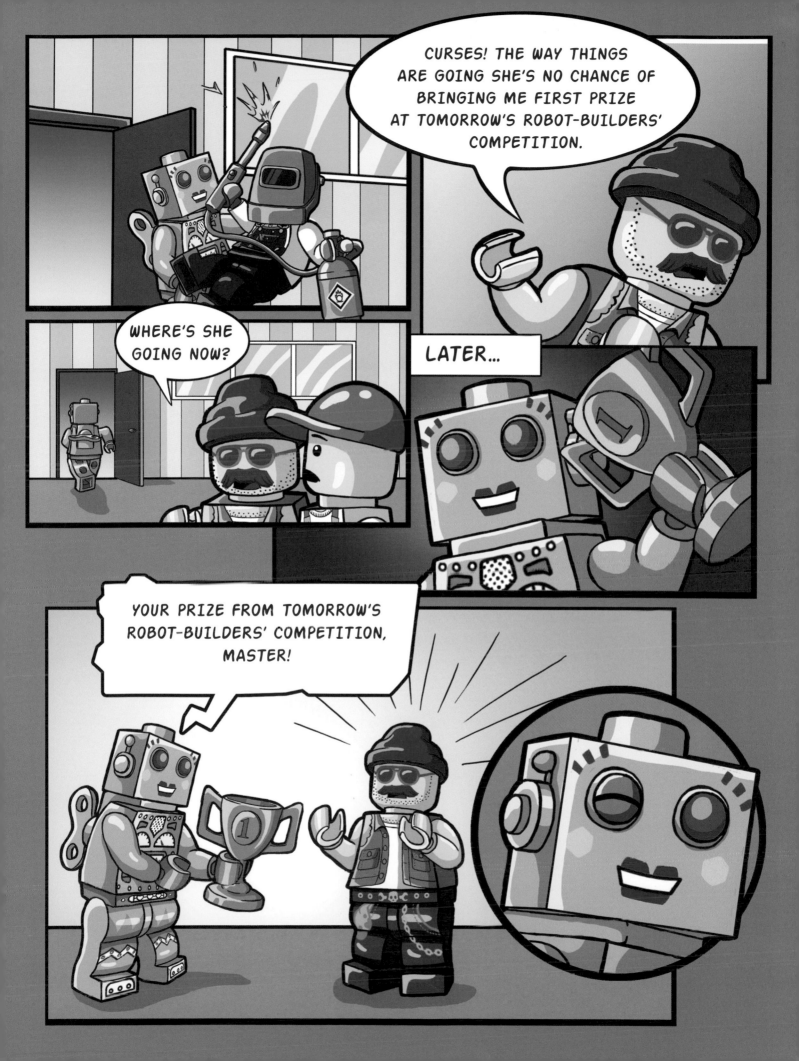

Parachute Plummet

Oh no! The Minifigures are having a parachuting contest, but Skydiver's parachute hasn't opened properly. Quickly draw the rest of his parachute, using the grid lines to help you. Then count all the parachutists in the picture and write the sum in the empty box.

Mix and Match

On the page opposite are loads of Minifigure accessories.
Some belong to the characters on this page, some don't.
Can you match the Minifigures to their belongings?

Ancient Code

Barbarian is delivering a top secret coded message to Island Warrior. What could it possibly be? See if you can figure it out.

O T I E C L W

D G M A Y Z K

Yeti's Trail

This pair of mountain climbers are on the trail of the most reclusive creature of all – the Yeti! That's him enjoying an ice lolly at the top of the mountain.
Can you find the route that will lead the adventurers to their hairy prize?

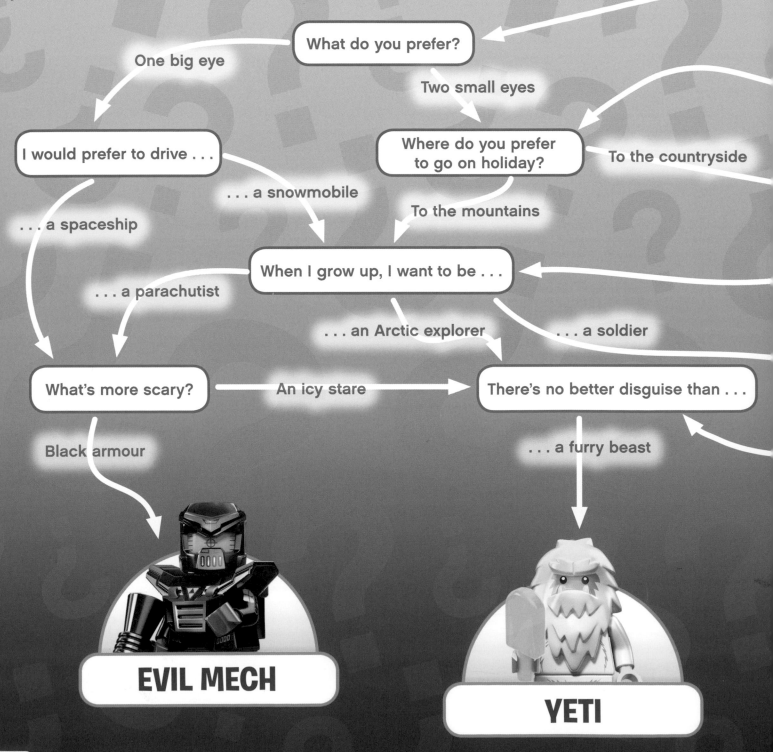

LEGO minifigures

Costume Party

You've been invited to the Minifigure fancy dress party! Hurray!
But what should you dress up as? Answer these questions to find out
your ideal outfit.

What do you prefer?

One big eye

Two small eyes

I would prefer to drive . . .

Where do you prefer to go on holiday?

To the countryside

. . . a snowmobile

To the mountains

. . . a spaceship

When I grow up, I want to be . . .

. . . a parachutist

. . . an Arctic explorer

. . . a soldier

What's more scary?

An icy stare

There's no better disguise than . . .

Black armour

. . . a furry beast

EVIL MECH

YETI

START

What's better – a funny or scary disguise?

Definitely funny!

Both funny and scary!

Definitely scary!

If you were a superhero, would you prefer to . . .

I think up new games

What do you do when you're bored?

. . . be really strong

. . . be a master of disguise

I help out at home

. . . have a great aim

When you're hungry, you reach for . . .

. . . with friends?

Do you prefer playing . . .

. . . ice cream

. . . chicken wings

. . . alone?

. . . a sandwich

What should a great costume be?

. . . bought in a shop

Your spooky costume should be . . .

Furry

Historical

. . . homemade

Scary but practical!

REVOLUTIONARY SOLDIER

SCARECROW

Shadow Wheel

This cheeky Holiday Elf just can't stop playing pranks on the other Minifigures! This time, he's jumbled up their shadows. How far round does the outer wheel need to move so that they are all back next to their own shadows?

Special Delivery

Roman Commander has just received a delivery of brand new shields.
So why does he look so unhappy? Well, they were all meant to be the same as his,
but four of them aren't. Put an 'x' underneath the four that are making him grumpy.

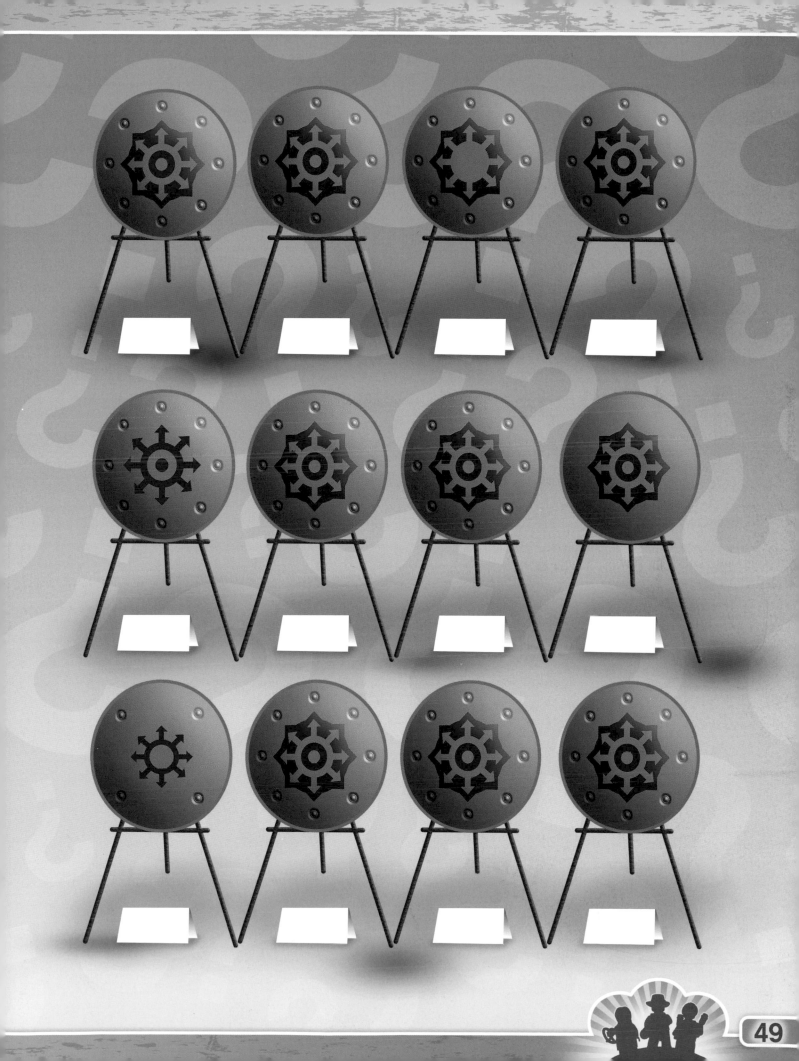

Awards Night

These Minifigures have been given an award for their new smash-hit movie, "Yeti vs. Gingerbread Man". Here they are, posing for a photo on the red carpet. Three of the photographs on the page opposite are different to the original. Can you spot which ones?

In the Lab . . .

This top scientist is about to carry out a very important experiment.
She has to mix different colours together and note down what happens.
Help her record her results by writing the correct number on each of her notes.

Elf Service

That pesky Holiday Elf is back, and this time he's giving out presents! Awesome! There's just one catch. He's only put goodies inside the ones that add up to an even number. Add up the numbers on each box to work out which ones are the real gifts.

Answers

p. 4 Odd Squad

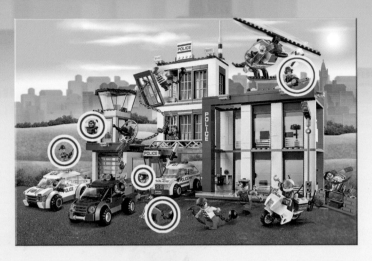

p. 6 Drive Time

p. 8 On Guard!

p. 10 Mechanic Panic

p. 14 Flame Game

p. 18 Arctic Drop-Off

p. 24 Dragon's Gold

Number of coins

12

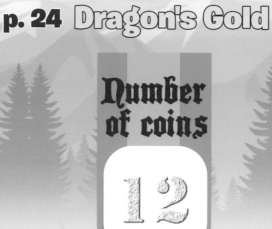

p. 20 Icy Cargo

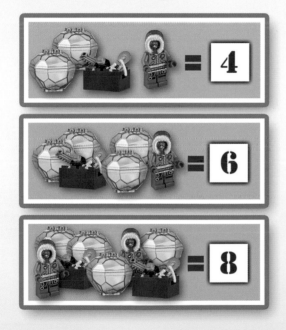

p. 26 Ambush!

4

p. 28 Under Siege

p. 22 Stolen Treasure

4

Welcome to LEGO City

p. 48 Special Delivery

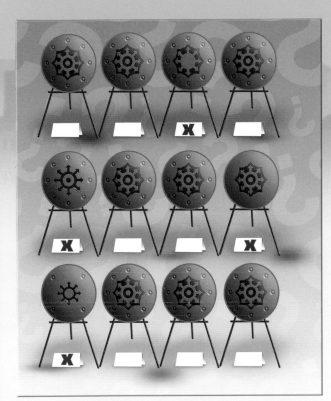

p. 52 In the Lab . . .

p. 50 Awards Night

p. 54 Elf Service

2 + 4 = 6

1 + 6 = 7

2 + 7 = 9

5 + 1 = 6

4 + 3 = 7

5 + 3 = 8